Bad NO MORE

25 Steps to Break ANY Bad Habit

By S.J. Scott

www.HabitBooks.com

Bad Habits No More Copyright © 2014 by S.J. Scott

All rights reserved. No part of this book may be reproduced in any form without permission in writing from the author. Reviewers may quote brief passages in reviews.

ISBN: 1505382858
ISBN-13: 978-1505382853

Disclaimer

No part of this publication may be reproduced or transmitted in any form or by any means, mechanical or electronic, including photocopying or recording, or by any information storage and retrieval system, or transmitted by email without permission in writing from the publisher.

While all attempts have been made to verify the information provided in this publication, neither the author nor the publisher assumes any responsibility for errors, omissions, or contrary interpretations of the subject matter herein.

This book is for entertainment purposes only. The views expressed are those of the author alone, and should not be taken as expert instruction or commands. The reader is responsible for his or her own actions.

Adherence to all applicable laws and regulations, including international, federal, state, and local governing professional licensing, business practices, advertising, and all other aspects of doing business in the US, Canada, or any other jurisdiction is the sole responsibility of the purchaser or reader.

Neither the author nor the publisher assumes any responsibility or liability whatsoever on the behalf of the purchaser or reader of these materials.

Any perceived slight of any individual or organization is purely unintentional.

Your Free Gift

As a way of saying *thanks* for your purchase, I'm offering a free report that's exclusive to my book and blog readers.

Lifelong habit development *isn't* easy for most people. The trick is to identify what you'd like to fix and create a step-by-step strategy to make that change. The key is to know *where to start*.

In *77 Good Habits to Live a Better Life*, you'll discover a variety of routines that can help you in many different areas of your life. You will learn how to make lasting changes to your work, success, learning, health and sleep habits.

This lengthy PDF (over 12,000 words) reviews each habit and provides a simple action plan. You can download this free report by going to the link below.

http://www.developgoodhabits.com/FREE

Table of Contents

Your Free Gift 4

Want to Break a Bad Habit? 8

The Myth of Willpower 11

PART I: PLAYING THE FOUNDATION FOR A HABIT CHANGE 14

    Step #1: Know the Difference between Bad Habits and Addictions 15

    Step #2: Focus on One Habit at a Time 18

    Step #3: Commit to a 30-Day Habit Challenge 21

    Step #4: Set a Start Date 26

    Step #5: Identify the Target Goal 27

    Step #6: Avoid Cold Turkey Solutions 29

    Step #7: Set a Baseline Metric 33

    Step #8: Create Incremental Goals (Optional) 35

PART II: UNDERSTAND YOUR HABIT LOOP ...37

Step #9: Identify the Habit Routine..................................38

Step #10: Record the Habit Triggers 40

Step #11: Try Different Rewards......................................43

Step #12: See What Works 46

Step #13: Create an "If-Then Plan".................................48

Step #14: Use "Habit Reminders" to Stay Consistent ..51

PART III: BUILD A SUPPORT SYSTEM.................53

Step #15: Keep an Accountability Journal............54

Step #16: Make a Public Declaration...............................56

Step #17: Find an Accountability Partner 59

Step #18: Ignore the Naysayers 61

Step #19: Avoid Trigger Locations 64

PART IV: OVERCOME CHALLENGES.................65

Step #20: Maintain a Healthy Lifestyle and Attitude.....66

Step #21: Beware the "What-the-Hell Effect" 68

Step #22: Practice Streaking 70

Step #23: Forgive Yourself..73

Step #24: Celebrate "Small Wins" 75

Step #25: Focus on the Journey, Not the Destination .. 77

Final Thoughts… 79

Would You Like to Know More 81

Did You Like *Bad Habits No More?* 82

More Books by Steve 83

Want to Break a Bad Habit?

Habits run our lives. Much of what you do is based on a habit you've developed at some point in your life. In fact, according to a 2006 study conducted at Duke University (http://cdp.sagepub.com/content/15/4/198.abstract), over 40 percent of what you do on a daily basis is habitual. In other words, you often complete the same actions, in the same place and at the same time.

Many habits are helpful, like eating healthy, exercising regularly and giving that "second glance" before switching lanes in a car.

Other habits are harmful, like smoking, drinking excessively or spending too much time on the Internet.

You might consider these routines to be nothing more than small hindrances, but some can have a long-term, debilitating impact on your life.

Since you're reading this book, I'll assume you want to break a specific bad habit. Odds are, you've tried in the past and maybe you were successful for a few days. Then something unexpected came up where you slipped for a day or two. One mistake snowballs into a series of setbacks. Eventually you give up on the idea of making a habit change simply because it's too difficult to do.

The interesting thing?

We've all experienced this pattern at some point in our lives.

You want to change a behavior, yet you keep experiencing failure. It doesn't mean you're lazy or weak-willed. It means you didn't have the right tools for making a lasting habit change.

What you need (and what the following book provides) is a strategy for identifying your worst habits and learning how to overcome them. I call it *Bad Habits No More: 25 Steps to Break ANY Bad Habit.*

This book wasn't written to lecture you about your mistakes. Nor is it designed to fill your head with rah-rah motivational nonsense where I tell you to simply "try a little harder." Instead, we'll talk about how to understand the *whys* behind a negative behavior and how to build positive habits to help you overcome it.

As you'll see, I don't believe in the idea of "white-knuckling" your way through a behavior change. This strategy rarely works because it doesn't teach you how to cope with temptations and moments of weakness.

Another thing you'll discover is the underlying psychology behind your bad habit. You perform every action for a specific reason, but rarely do you take the time to fully understand your behavior. With this book, you'll learn how to explore your feelings while engaged in a bad habit and then create an action plan for when temptations pile up.

Bad Habits No More is designed to be an action plan. I've eliminated all unnecessary fluff. I've kept each step short and to the point. And I've included a case study (from my life) that best illustrates the logic behind each piece of advice. The goal here is to provide you with a book that can be read in under an hour and then immediately applied to your life.

Who Am I?

My name is Steve "S.J." Scott. I run the blog *Develop Good Habits* (http://www.developgoodhabits.com/) and I'm the author of a series of habit-related titles, all of which are available at www.HabitBooks.com.

The purpose of my content is to show how *continuous* habit development can lead to a better life. Instead of lecturing you, I provide simple strategies that are easy to use no matter how busy you are. It's been my experience that the best way to make a lasting change is to develop one quality habit at a time.

Like you, I've struggled with certain bad habits. While I've never had to deal with a major addiction (like smoking, drinking or gambling), I definitely have my fair share of routines that don't add value to my life (like snacking on junk food or engaging in pointless activities).

Eventually, I realized that all bad habits share a similar pattern. The trick, I found, is to understand this pattern and know how to take a series of actions to eliminate negative behaviors.

Bad Habits No More is the result of my experiences. It's a collection of different lessons I've learned about overcoming bad habits.

We'll start with a brief discourse on the dangers of relying on willpower. Then we'll move into the 25 steps for overcoming a bad habit. Each step includes a short case study to show you how I applied this information to break a small (but time-consuming) habit in June 2014.

This book covers a lot of ground in a short amount of time, so let's dive in by talking about a common myth many people have about habit development.

The Myth of Willpower

All conversations about habit development should start with a discussion of "willpower." This is a phrase we use whenever we try to break negative routines. In fact, we often blame a lack of willpower when things do not go according to plan. After failing, we usually say something like, "I didn't have the willpower to resist temptation."

The truth is people place too much emphasis on willpower. Sure it's important to follow through with our commitments, but it's only one piece of the puzzle.

Breaking a habit isn't a simple matter of grinding your way through the day and swearing to never succumb to temptation. If you rely on mental strength alone, then you won't know how to act when you're overwhelmed by stress or mental exhaustion.

When you attempt to change a habit, failure stems from a concept called "ego depletion."

In the book *Willpower* (http://www.developgoodhabits.com/willpower) by Roy F. Baumeister and John Tierney, the authors describe ego depletion as **"a person's diminished capacity to regulate their thoughts, feelings, and actions."**

Simply put, your willpower is like a muscle–it weakens throughout the day because of constant use. You also have a limited amount of willpower. Once you reach your limit, it becomes *very* difficult to focus and resist temptations.

Ego depletion has been tested in a number of other experiments, producing findings similar to those of Baumeister and his colleagues.

They have proven two important things:

1. You have a finite amount of willpower that becomes depleted as you use it.
2. You use the same stock of willpower for every type of task.

This has an important implication when it comes to breaking bad habits. Your life is already filled with stress, obligations and a lot of decisions. Each withdraws a small amount of your willpower. As the day goes on, you'll find it gets increasingly difficult to regulate your behavior and stay committed to a habit change. (And that's why most of us "binge" on bad habits late in the evening.)

Now let's toss another concept into the mix.

At some point, we've all experienced what's called the "hot-cold empathy gap." The official Wikipedia (http://en.wikipedia.org/wiki/Empathy_gap) definition of the hot-cold empathy gap (or HCEG) is as follows:

"A cognitive bias in which a person underestimates the influences of visceral drives, and instead attributes behavior primarily to other, non visceral factors."

In layman's terms, whenever we plan a habit change, it's easy to underestimate the level of desire or temptation we experience on a regular basis.

Even worse, when you fail to plan for those moments of weakness, it's easy to turn a simple temptation into a snowball effect that results in binging on a bad habit.

Let's say you want to lose weight, so you plan to overhaul your diet. You promise to eat healthy greens and follow a gluten-free, no-processed-food diet for the rest of your life. It's fun to write down this goal because you're making a commitment to create a better version of yourself.

This plan works great for a few days. You've dropped a few pounds and you experience a new level of energy. But one day your boss yells at you because of an error on the TPS report. Suddenly your willpower is starting to crack. You feel bad about yourself, so all you want now is some comfort food—like a few slices of delicious pizza. Next thing you know, you're sitting at home, gorging on an extra-large pizza pie with *all* the fixings.

And what about your new diet? It's quickly forgotten because you're tired, stressed and simply want to feel better.

This is an extreme form of the HCEG. When you mapped out your new habit, you didn't plan for those times when ego depletion pops up and you experience a heightened amount of temptation.

The truth is, our best intentions often fail in the harsh light of **how much you desire to engage in the very habit you're trying to eliminate**. In psychology terms, your super-ego is no match for your id.

People tend to make promises (like on New Year's Eve) that they can't keep when faced with temptation. Even worse, they *forget* how alluring certain impulses feel.

When planning a habit change, expect to face temptation, especially when your willpower is at its weakest. Only when you understand your own limitations will you have a plan for overcoming them.

With that in mind, let's jump into the step-by-step portion of this book, starting with laying the foundation for making a specific habit change.

PART I:

LAYING THE FOUNDATION FOR A HABIT CHANGE

Step #1: Know the Difference between Bad Habits and Addictions

It's important to start with an extreme example of bad habits—addictions.

Frankly, it's easy to fall into the trap of lying to ourselves about a negative routine. You might think an action (like drinking) is an innocent thing that "sometimes" gets out of control. However, the people around you might have a different opinion. Perhaps they feel this habit is the sign of a deep-seated addiction that needs immediate attention.

To be honest, you can only break *some* habits by following the plan in this book. Others are the result of addictions that might require you to seek out professional counseling or join an organization that has a strong support system.

Do you have an addiction?

The following questions will help you determine the true answer.

Do you:

1. Experience withdrawal symptoms when you stop doing the behavior (e.g. lack of focus, anger, frustration or insomnia)?
2. Stop doing the activities you once found enjoyable to engage in this habit instead?
3. Go on binges whenever you do the habit?

4. Keep a stash or supply of the product for emergencies (i.e. hiding bottles of alcohol throughout your home)?
5. Obsess about doing the activity to the point where it interferes with your daily routine?
6. Have financial difficulties because you've spent all of your money on the activity?
7. Have trouble limiting the activity? For instance, one pint turns into a binge-drinking session that ends with you blacking out.
8. Have health issues directly related to this activity?
9. Engage in risky behavior whenever doing this activity?
10. Do the activity as a way to deal with stress and emotional problems?
11. Deny or hide your behavior from others?
12. Damage your interpersonal relationships because of this activity?

People who suffer from alcoholism, drug addiction, binge eating, chain smoking and eating disorders usually experience some or all of these symptoms. It's not an all-or-nothing checklist, so if you read it and some of the scenarios sound familiar, then you might want to seek out a professional solution to your possible addiction.

Here are few ways to do this:

- Talk to a psychologist or psychiatrist who specializes in addictions.
- Join a group like NA (Narcotics Anonymous) or AA (Alcoholics Anonymous).
- Join a weight-loss group that emphasizes permanent life changes instead of fad diets.

- Ask your doctor about different (non-addictive) ways to battle cravings.

Don't be afraid to seek help from others. You might have an addiction that you can't overcome by following a simple checklist. Odds are, if you *think* you have a real problem, then it might be time to get the assistance you really need.

Step #2: Focus on One Habit at a Time

Now it's time to *prepare* for the habit change. Odds are you've tried to break this routine in the past. In all likelihood, you failed because you didn't have a plan or relied too much on willpower.

Failure in the past doesn't mean you'll fail in the future. Usually it's a direct result of not having a solid strategy for overcoming the habit. In other words, you didn't follow that age-old adage:

"When you fail to plan, you plan to fail."

So, before anything else, take time to understand what you're giving up; then plan for the resistance you'll experience along the way.

This goes back to the conversation about ego depletion. Remember—you have a limited amount of willpower every day. When it's depleted, it's hard to control your impulses.

An important part of this plan is to focus on changing one habit at a time. Think of the New Year's resolutions many people make. They usually start the year with a lengthy list of habits they'd like change. Instead of focusing on one behavior, they try to fix their entire lives—all on the first of January.

People who make New Year's resolutions typically fail because it's almost impossible to change multiple habits at the same time. Most don't have the willpower necessary to manage multiple new routines. As a result, one failure often snowballs into multiple failures when someone attempts to juggle several new routines at the same time. It's not unusual for people to get so frustrated with one new routine that they give up on *all* their new routines.

My point?

Even if you want to change multiple areas of your life, it's best to commit to one habit change at a time. That way, you can focus all your mental energy on making one change. In the next step, you'll learn how to do this.

CASE STUDY

As I mentioned in the introduction, the best way to explain the steps in this book is to give you specific examples of how I implemented each step to eliminate a habit I once engaged in on a daily basis.

Like many people, I spend a lot of time on the Internet and immersed in the digital world in general. This is usually a positive habit because it helps me maintain a high level of productivity; however, I eventually developed the bad habit of spending too much time on my cellphone when I wasn't in front of a computer. By scanning email, looking at business stats, reading pointless "click bait" articles or checking social media, I once wasted a lot of my time on my cellphone.

In May 2014, I read a great article (http://www.rowdykittens.com/2010/07/digital-sabbatical/) about the idea of taking "digital sabbaticals." The idea here is to dedicate a day every week (or month) to completely unplug from the digital world. While I frequently do this during the summertime, I decided to take this idea and create a **"cellphone sabbatical habit"** where I completely disconnect for most of the day.

Obviously, this is a vague outcome that's almost impossible to track. But as you'll see later in the book, I was able narrow down this concept and turn it into an actionable strategy. As a result, I no longer fiddle around my phone when I'm trying to relax.

Step #3: Commit to a 30-Day Habit Challenge

There's conflicting information about how long it takes to make a lasting habit change. Many people believe it takes 21 days, but a study (http://onlinelibrary.wiley.com/doi/10.1002/ejsp.674/abstract) by Phillippa Lally and her research team showed it takes 66 days to create a brand-new routine.

My opinion is it takes **a least** a month to break a bad habit, so a great way to get started is to commit to a 30-day habit challenge (30DHC).

The 30DHC doesn't come from a specific scientific study. Instead, it's something I picked up from Steve Pavlina's website (http://www.stevepavlina.com/blog/2005/04/30-days-to-success/). He compares this concept to a trial version of software. You don't actually "buy into" the habit change until the end of the test period. Only then will you decide to keep it or ditch it.

As Pavlina says, **it's hard to get through those first few weeks of a habit change**. That's the time when most people succumb to their impulses. Once you get *past* this critical period, it becomes easier to stick to a new routine.

In a way, the 30DHC tricks your mind into forming a new habit. It's easy to do something unpleasant if you think it's *only* for a month. And when the time expires, you'll be close to making a permanent change.

The 30DHC also gives you an "out" if the new habit isn't working. At the end of the month, you can decide if it's worth continuing. That said, what usually happens is you want to maintain that momentum and keep going, even at the end of the 30-day period.

What I *really* like about the 30DHC is the confidence you gain. You know what it's like to follow a habit on a day-to-day basis, so you develop an intuitive understanding of both your *positive* and *negative* triggers. This information is important when you focus on improving your results.

To get started with the 30DHC, I recommend the following action plan:

(1*) Have a Reason Why

Start by journaling about this habit. Give a specific reason *why* it matters. What you write is irrelevant. The important thing is to know why you want to make this change and what result you expect from this experience.

(2*) Obstacles

Every habit has a *trigger*. This is a thought, cue or action that makes you want to do the bad habit. Your job is to identify any trigger that pops up.

Use your journal to track triggers by writing them as they occur. Include the following important information: *Where are you? Who is with you? What are you doing? What thoughts are in your head?*

This data is very important for eliminating the bad habit and replacing it with something positive. (We'll talk more about this in a later step.)

(3*) Action Plan

Write down an overview of the habit, along with the step-by-step actions you'll take. Be sure to include any tools or environmental cues that will help or hinder your completion of this new routine.

(4*) Results

Track your success with a <u>daily metric</u>. The tool I use is Lift.do (http://lift.do/), which tracks all my current habits.

You can track a habit in a variety of ways:

- Yes or No (Did you do it today or not?)
- Quantity (How many times did you complete the habit?)
- Number (Are you over or under the set "quota"?)
- Time (How long did you spend on this habit every day?)

Using the daily metric is the key to forming a permanent habit. There <u>will be</u> days where you'll *fall off the wagon*. The important thing is to track these lapses and carry on.

(5*) Verdict

You'll need to make a decision at the end of the month: *Should it stay or should it go?*

Analyze this habit. *Did it help your life? Can you improve the process? Did you have time to complete it? Should you keep it, or should you eliminate it? Should you try it for another 30 days and see what happens?*

It's important to make a decision after 30 days.

I recommend doing one of three things: (1) Keep It: Continue to track this habit on a daily basis. Try to turn it into a permanent change. (2) Ditch It: The habit didn't work for some reason, so stop doing it. (3) Tweak It: Some habit changes won't work because you created a bad *process*. Change the routine and try it again.

CASE STUDY

In June 2014, I made the decision to reduce (not eliminate) the amount of time I spent on my cellphone. Here's how I initiated this habit change with a 30DHC:

#1. Reason Why: *Improving my quality of life* was the primary motivator for reducing the amount of time spent on my cellphone. I'm good about not looking at my cellphone while I'm working, but I had a tendency to slip early in the morning and late in the evening. These were the times I was supposed to relaxing, yet I'd spend time browsing websites and looking at things that didn't truly matter to me. By reducing time spent on my cellphone, I hoped to have more free time for the fun things in life.

#2. Obstacles: Early on, I realized that my main trigger was boredom. In the morning, I wasn't ready to start the day, so I'd procrastinate by spending time on my cellphone. In the evening, I'd use my cellphone if I was bored by a TV show or particular activity. Instead of finding an engaging activity to do, I used my cellphone as a crutch to break the monotony.

#3. Action Plan: My solution was a simple, but very effective. At the end of my workday, I would put my phone on the charger in my office, then close the door and refuse to touch it until the morning. In essence, this created a block of time (generally from 7 p.m. to 7 a.m.) where I would have a 12-hour cellphone sabbatical.

When starting out, there were a few "what ifs" that went through my mind:

What if I wanted to read a Kindle book?

The solution was to buy a Kindle Paperwhite and use it do all my reading. I chose this low-tech approach because you can't surf the Internet with this device.

What if I had to check something important online?

The solution was to use my laptop if I really had to look something up. I chose this option because it was a hassle—I'd have to turn my computer on and then a wait a few minutes for it to load up. This helped me quickly determine whether I really needed to look up something right then and there, or if it was just an impulse.

What if I needed to wake up early in the morning?

The solution was to use an amazing piece of technology called an "alarm clock." Yes, they still make these devices.

What if someone called (or texted) me with an emergency?

My phone has a loud ringer, and I'm a light sleeper. And honestly, who really texts someone when there's a legitimate emergency?

Ultimately, I discovered these excuses were nothing more than that—excuses. We often trick ourselves into not taking action because we think the obstacles are insurmountable. But when you apply a bit of logic, you'll discover simple solutions to pretty much any problem.

#4. Results: I used a simple "yes or no" metric to track this habit. In June, I successfully completed the cellphone sabbatical habit 29 out of 30 times.

More importantly, I got more out of my life in that month. I wasn't stressed by looking at email or my to-do list. I was more engaged in conversations with the people around me. Finally, I was able to read more books and get more exercise.

#5. Verdict: Keep it! While I haven't been 100 percent consistent with this habit since June, I still know that at the end of the workday, my cellphone goes in the office and I don't touch it until the morning.

Step #4: Set a Start Date

Write down the date when you'll start this habit change. It's important to take this goal seriously, so having an official "countdown" will help you stay on track. You should also tell friends and family members about this goal to get their support. (More on this later.)

Having a start date creates energy and excitement for this new change. Your aim is to dramatically improve your life, so you should feel energized about the countdown.

In the previous section we talked about doing a challenge for 30 days, so you might be tempted to wait until the start of the next month. My advice? Start as soon as possible. Sure, it won't be a full month, but the important thing is you're taking immediate action.

CASE STUDY

Technically, I started the cellphone sabbatical in the last week of May. However, I didn't start tracking it until June 1, 2014.

Step #5: Identify the Target Goal

Eliminating a bad habit is like setting a goal. You won't achieve it without having a specific outcome in mind coupled with a target date.

For instance, you can't say, *"I want to eat healthier."* Instead, you need to identify what foods to eat, what foods to avoid and the date when this change will happen.

The following would be a better goal: *"On August 1, I will no longer eat fast food from places like McDonald's or Burger King. Instead, I will eat home-cooked meals that combine vegetables with lean protein and unrefined carbohydrates."*

Notice how this outcome has a deadline with a specific outcome. By August 1, you'll know if it's working or not. That's how you set a goal for breaking a habit.

Since we're emphasizing a 30-day trial period, I recommend you create some sort of metric for the end of the month. Then when date arrives, you can decide if you want to continue with the habit change.

CASE STUDY

My target goal for the cellphone sabbatical was as follows:

"On July 1, I will have put my cellphone in my office from 7 a.m. to 7 p.m. each day for at least 25 days in the previous month."

Although I gave myself a few day of wiggle room, I quickly realized the importance of consistency, so I continued to do it even when I knew I'd surpass my initial goal. As you'll learn later on, developing streaks for your new habit is a great way to stay consistent.

Step #6: Avoid Cold Turkey Solutions

Let's me start by clarifying something—many behavioral experts will disagree with what I'm about to tell you. The reason I recommend this step is because many people depend way too much on "all-or-nothing" solutions when it comes to habit changes. But what I've found most effective in my personal life (and when talking to others who are into personal development) is the best long-term results come from making gradual changes in your life.

My advice is to avoid going "cold turkey" on your bad habit. Instead, it's better to focus on making small changes that compound over time.

Here's why…

We've all tried the cold turkey solution before. You promise you'll never do a bad habit again. A few days later, you're doing the *exact* routine you swore you'd eliminate forever.

True, quitting cold turkey *sometimes* works. We all know someone who gave up smoking or drinking through sheer force of will without falling off the wagon. But for every success story, there are hundreds of people who try the cold turkey solution and experience complete failure.

The main problem with cold turkey is the overemphasis on *perfection*.

Most people have this negative mindset:
One mistake = FAILURE!

Nobody is perfect. Having a goal of **never again** leaves you with no wiggle room when you cave into the temptation of doing the bad habit. Trust me, we all slip from time to time, so focusing on perfection is *not* the way to change a routine.

Going cold turkey can even make a bad habit worse. When people have insist on 100 percent perfection, they often develop a "what the hell" mindset when making a mistake. This is a phenomenon that's related to the hot-cold empathy gap we discussed in the section about willpower.

Think about those times when you're trying to only eat healthy foods. One day, a slice of pizza starts calling to you. *"Eat me, eat me!"* the pizza is practically screaming, so your willpower snaps and you eat one slice.

What usually happens at this point? Do you count it as a mistake and jump right back into your diet? Not usually.

For most dieters, the response is something like this: *"What the hell. I've already made a mistake, so I might as well enjoy my failure."*

In essence, if you try to go cold turkey, there is a good chance the "what–the-hell effect" will rear its ugly head. Once this happens, you might slip into a bizarre behavior pattern resulting in complete failure.

This often happens when people go on a diet. Numerous experiments have shown that when someone on a calorie-restricted diet goes over their "limit," they are far more likely to over-indulge than someone who is *not* dieting.

Anyone who has dieted in the past can think of a time where they blew their diet in a spectacular manner. (One of the reasons "*diet*" is considered a bad word by many nutritionists is because it focuses on short-term changes instead of modifying the underlying behavior.)

As we talked about before, willpower is like a muscle. It doesn't have an on or off switch. Instead, it's built and strengthened through constant use. It can also wear out and become fatigued. Everything you do that requires willpower weakens your resolve and increases the likelihood that your willpower will break down the next time you try to use it.

The point? It's easier to chunk down a habit change into small actions. That way, you're not drawing too much from your overtaxed willpower. The idea here is to create small wins that build emotional momentum, which helps you prevent those spectacular failures that often happen with cold turkey solutions.

As an example, it's impossible to overhaul your entire diet in a single month. What you could do *instead* is focus on a small aspect of your diet for the next 30 days, like not eating at a fast food restaurant. Then when you've eliminated this habit, you can chip away at the other negative aspects of your diet.

Later on, we'll talk about how to deal with the "what-the-hell effect." For now, though, I recommend you avoid the all-or-nothing approach of a cold turkey solution.

CASE STUDY

Notice how I said I'd *minimize* the cellphone habit, not eliminate it entirely? By studying my own behavior, I determined that the worst times I overused my cellphone were in the early morning and in the late evening. I gave myself a "free pass" to use my cellphone at other times during the day.

Surprisingly, I get so busy during the workday, the thought of checking my cellphone rarely occurs to me.

Did you also notice how, when I started this habit in June, I gave myself a bit of wiggle room on the total number of days (25 out of 30)? That way, I had a little cushion for those occasions when I slipped up. This is the kind of attitude you'll need to successfully break a bad habit.

Step #7: Set a Baseline Metric

The best way to make a permanent change is to focus on daily, incremental improvements. Your aim is to wean yourself from the habit by setting target goals that consistently decrease the amount of time you spend on it.

It all starts with a baseline metric. This metric can vary according to the specific habit you're trying to change:

- A daily "yes" or "no" for eating fast food
- The number of cigarettes smoked every day
- The number of times each day you bite your fingernails
- How much you currently weigh
- The number of calories you consume on a daily basis
- How many drinks you consume while "going out"
- The amount of time spent on Facebook or surfing the Internet
- The amount of time spent watching television

Knowledge is power. The more information you have about a habit, the easier it is to completely eliminate it.

CASE STUDY

The metric for the cellphone sabbatical was a simple "yes" or "no" question. Either I put my cellphone away for the day or I didn't. As you can see, some habits don't need a large amount of tracking.

Step #8: Create Incremental Goals (Optional)

As we've discussed, some bad habits are a "yes" or "no" proposition—either you do them or you don't. With other ones, it's all about the amount of usage. With these habits, going cold turkey isn't a realistic long-term goal. Instead, it's better to create incremental goals where you slowly move away from the bad habit.

EXAMPLE:

Let's say you're a smoker who averages 20 cigarettes a day. Your ultimate goal is to completely eliminate this habit. But for now, you'd stick to these incremental goals:

- 15 cigarettes each day for weeks 1 to 3
- 10 cigarettes each day for weeks 4 to 6
- 5 cigarettes each day for weeks 7 to 9
- 3 cigarettes each day for weeks 10 to 12
- 1 (or fewer) cigarettes each day for weeks 13 and beyond

Obviously, your numbers will be different, and there will be times when you'll fail with this goal. The key here is to make *slow, steady changes* to your life. Breaking a habit in a methodical manner gives your body and mind a chance to diminish their constant cravings.

The question is this: *How do distract yourself from the cravings associated with this habit?*

A simple answer is to replace them. In the next section, we'll talk about how to identify your bad habit triggers and what to do when they pop up. Once you start weaning yourself off the habit, you want to replace it with a new, healthier activity.

CASE STUDY

I didn't use incremental goals for the cellphone sabbatical. Instead, I focused on building the habit of leaving the cellphone in my office for the 12-hour period and resisting the urge to check it during the evening hours.

PART II:

UNDERSTAND YOUR HABIT LOOP

Step #9: Identify the Habit Routine

Determining how much time you spend on a habit is a mentally exhausting activity. In fact, it often acts as a constant reminder of what you're giving up. So the secret for forever eliminating this behavior is to identify its habit loops and understand the underlying motivations of *why* you do it on a regular basis.

In his book, *The Power of Habit* (http://www.developgoodhabits.com/power-of-habit-review/), Charles Duhigg talks about "habit loops," which are the actions that bring you from *cue* to *reward*. If you understand these actions, you'll take that first step toward making a permanent lifestyle change.

The best way to forever eliminate a habit is to slowly replace or "imprint" negative habits with healthier routines. That means instead of focusing on what you're missing, you'll follow new routines that give you the same reward.

Once you've scheduled a "start date," you'll want to take time to understand the three-step pattern of your habit:

1. **The Cue:** A situational trigger based on a reward you're seeking.
2. **The Reward:** The satisfaction you seek by following the routine.

3. **The Routine:** A physical or emotional action you take to obtain the reward.

To illustrate this concept, check out this PDF flowchart Duhigg offers on his blog: http://bit.ly/1rTO6Jr

All habits have *actions* and *thoughts* that occur beforehand. The **cue** is the trigger that creates a craving to get a reward. The **reward** is the satisfaction you feel from following this routine, or it's the removal of stress created by the cute. The **routine** is the action you take to satisfy this impulse.

The best way to understand this process is to go over each of the individual components, so we'll go over each of the key components in the next few steps.

CASE STUDY

It took a while to figure out why I had the urge to check my cellphone. Eventually, I was able to break it out into a typical pattern:

#1. The Cue: My urge started with an impulse to check some aspect of my business. It was often triggered by a thought such as "I wonder how ___ is doing?" In a way, I experienced a level of anxiety that was only relieved by looking at a webpage on my cellphone.

#2. The Reward: My reward was usually a straightforward one—I felt less anxious once I looked at a page and realized "everything is okay." (**Side note**: One of the downsides to being an entrepreneur is it's hard to turn off your brain and *not* think about your business.)

#3: The Routine: It usually followed a similar pattern. I'd check a certain page (Kindle book sales, reviews, traffic stats, optimization tests or my email inbox.) Then I'd check the weather, CNN.com or Facebook. Then 30 minutes later, I'd end up watching a trashy video like *"He Tried to Pet a Cat. What Happened Next Will SHOCK YOU."*

(Admit it—we all fall for these inane videos from time to time.)

Step #10: Record the Habit Triggers

We are constantly bombarded with cues to take certain actions. Sometimes they're external (a sight, sound or smell creates a craving). Other times, it's an internal sensation that sparks this desire.

To make a *permanent* change, you need to fully understand *when* and *why* these "triggers" occur. You can easily do this by **recording five pieces of information** whenever you feel the need to engage in a bad habit:

1. **Location:** Record where you are.
2. **Time:** Write down the exact time when you felt the urge.
3. **Mood:** Record your emotional state and what you're thinking.
4. **People:** Who is with you or who is around you?
5. **Action:** What did you just do? What are you currently doing?

The key to this exercise is *repetition*. Focus on recording these five data points in the first few weeks of the new habit change. Do this for at least a week and you'll notice a consistent pattern to your behavior.

EXAMPLE:

Let's say you're trying to curb your consumption of alcohol. On the surface, it might seem like an innocent activity, but this drinking habit has led to a number of problems: arguments at home, decreased productivity and even a DUI last month. Now a once-fun activity has morphed into a serious issue.

In addition to seeking help from others (like I described in step #1), you'd get insight on this habit by tracking its triggers. After careful recording, you notice that these five patterns stand out:

1. **Location:** O'Brien's Bar & Grille
2. **Time:** 3:00p.m.
3. **Mood:** Stressed out
4. **People:** With "The Guys" (Frank, Bill and Dave)
5. **Action:** Watching the baseball game

Your goal is to minimize your drinking. After tracking this habit for a few weeks, you realize that the problem most often occurs when you're stressed out or feel like hanging out with your buddies and watching the ballgame.

By analyzing these triggers, you now know that your drinking is caused by a desire to feel relaxed and reduce stress. More importantly, it's an activity you prefer to share with other people.

CASE STUDY

There were two primary triggers for my urge to check the cellphone:

Trigger 1:

1. **Location:** In bed
2. **Time:** 7 a.m. to 7:30 a.m.
3. **Mood:** Groggy, unenergetic. Wondering what happened with the business overnight.

4. **People:** By myself
5. **Action:** Just woke up.

Trigger 2:

1. **Location:** On the couch in my living room.
2. **Time:** 8 p.m.
3. **Mood:** Tired, bored.
4. **People:** My fiancée
5. **Action:** Just ate dinner, not sure what to do with the rest of the evening.

As you can see, these triggers practically bookended my day. In the morning, I felt a desire to see how things were going with the business; in the evening, I experienced the same impulse.

Step #11: Try Different Rewards

The interesting thing about bad habits is they often come from a desire to receive a subconscious reward. Usually we do them because we want to feel relaxed, happy, energized, accepted or loved.

The good news is you can substitute a bad habit with a new routine and *still* receive this positive benefit. The trick is to experiment with rewards and find one that produces the same subconscious reward.

EXAMPLE:

Let's go back to the example from before—consuming too much alcohol. After identifying triggers for a few days, you realize the drinking habit comes from a need to reduce stress and feel relaxed. It's also a byproduct of a desire to socialize and have fun.

So you can plan different strategies whenever you feel the need to relax:

- Going for a 10-minute walk around the neighborhood
- Avoiding O'Brien's Bar & Grille
- Doing a different activity with friends instead of drinking

- Making new connections and building up your social network
- Meditating for a half-hour

Not all of these strategies will be right for your situation, but this process is important because you're trying to find a new routine that provides a reward similar to the reward produced by the bad habit.

CASE STUDY

In the last step, I described how I had two separate triggers for my cellphone habit. In the morning, the urge popped up because I was groggy and not ready to start writing. In the evening, it was because I was bored. Since there were two triggers, I realized I had to create a substitute routine for both.

In the morning, I decided to start my **"habit-stacking routine"** (http://www.developgoodhabits.com/habit-stacking) 15 minutes earlier. Instead of "waking up" by looking at my cellphone, I committed to taking a quick walk as soon as I opened my eyes.

Early on, when building this new habit, I had to remind myself that the best way to feel awake was to get outside and start moving around. Only after I completed the habit-stacking routine did I allow myself to look at my cellphone. However, even that time was limited because I had to start my #1 habit—writing.

In the evening, I'd substitute the cellphone habit with activities that made me feel relaxed and less anxious: dinner conversation with my fiancée, reading, watching a good movie or taking a night walk. All of these activities were things I *already* enjoyed, yet I once convinced myself that I didn't have time to do them.

What's interesting is, immediately after replacing my cellphone habit, my urge to check it went away. That's because I was doing activities that helped me feel relaxed after a long workday.

Step #12: See What Works

The key to finding the best *replacement habit* is to examine your mood after completing a new routine to see if you *still* feel a desire to do the bad habit. If it's still there, then you know the replacement habit doesn't produce the reward you're seeking.

Let's go back to our drinking example.

You tried exercise and meditation, but neither reduced your stress levels. What *did* work was forming new friendships with people who don't spend their time in a bar. These positive people help you feel relaxed, which minimizes the tense feeling you experience before having a drink.

You also know that Dave (one of your buddies from O'Brien's Bar & Grille) loves hiking, which is an activity you also enjoy. This means you can minimize your drinking while staying connected to one of your friends.

Another thing you might notice is that *people* often trigger bad habits. That means you have to make a decision—either you spend less time around them or you keep repeating unhealthy behavior. Sure, it's not easy to "let go" of certain people, but sometimes you need to sacrifice relationships that typically lead to self-destructive habit loops.

CASE STUDY

In my first attempt to reduce cellphone usage, I tested a few things: tracking the time I used it, disabling certain apps and asking my fiancée to hide the phone every evening.

None of these worked because I wasn't resolving the underlying reasons of *why* I felt the urge to check my phone. I also discovered that when the phone was physically "put away," the impulse wasn't always there.

I ultimately chose the cellphone sabbatical solution because it gave me a simple choice: (a) Either I wasted time on an activity that didn't matter, or (b) I spent my time doing the things I personally enjoyed. I almost always made the right decision.

Step #13: Create an "If-Then Plan"

It often takes a few weeks of experimenting to find a replacement habit. Eventually, though, you'll find a routine that produces the same reward. When that happens, you should realign your mindset to focus on repeating this behavior instead of dwelling on the habit you're trying to eliminate.

The best way to make a lasting change is to follow a step-by-step plan whenever you experience that impulse to revert back to old behavior. You can do this by focusing on the triggers you identified from Step #10 and creating a plan for *each* one. The goal here is to reprogram your mind to take a different action, even when you feel that craving.

All of this is possible with an *if-then plan*.

This is a concept related to the Implementation Intention (http://en.wikipedia.org/wiki/Implementation_intention) experiments conducted by Peter Gollwitzer. In one experiment, Gollwitzer asked his students to mail in an assignment two days before Christmas. One group was simply given the assignment, while the other was asked to form specific if-then statements: *When would they mail the assignment? Where they would mail it? How they would mail it?*

The results?

The first group (no specific instructions) had a 32 percent success rate, and the second group (if-then instructions) had a 72 percent success rate. They more than doubled their success rate simply by having a plan.

If you want to successfully break a bad habit, then you need to create a series of if-then plans for those moments when you feel tempted to cave in to temptation.

Once again, let's go back to the drinking example. Here are a few new strategies you could implement:

"When Dave invites me to O'Brien's, I will suggest a hike instead."

"On 'Football Sunday,' I will attend Meetup.com activities instead of hitting the bar."

"At 5:00 every day, I will go for a 30-minute walk to reduce stress."

The idea here is to identify your "weak spots" and create a plan for how you'll act. This will be your first line of defense against a bad-habit impulse. Whenever a craving strikes, you'll know exactly what to do instead.

The point behind an if-then plan is to fully understand **when you typically fail** and then create a plan for what to do when that scenario pops up.

CASE STUDY

I was surprised at how often I felt compelled to check my cellphone. The trigger usually started as a random thought. When I didn't have an if-then plan, I often found myself automatically grabbing my phone without understanding *why* I was doing it.

To counteract this behavior, I came up with a few if-then plans to follow whenever the urge to check my phone popped up:

"If I feel like I need to check a certain webpage, I will write down a reminder to follow up when I'm using my laptop."

"If the urge happens while working, I will only check my phone when I've completed a block from the Pomodoro Technique" (http://pomodorotechnique.com/).

"If I absolutely have to check a webpage in the evening, I will do it on my laptop and stand up the entire time. That way, I won't get comfortable and end up wasting 30 minutes of my time."

As you can see, you can get pretty creative with making a plan around your triggers. The key (as we've discussed) is to fully understand your weaknesses and have a strategy in place for handling them.

Step #14: Use "Habit Reminders" to Stay Consistent

Habit reminders are a great way to build a new routine. Write these reminders down on a piece of paper you keep with you at all times, or add them as alerts on your cellphone. These reminders might seem silly, yet they act as a great catalyst to keep repeating your replacement habit.

My favorite habit reminder app is *Mind Jogger* (https://itunes.apple.com/us/app/mind-jogger/id409841508?mt=8), which uses reminders to keep you on track. I prefer this tool over the regular calendar app because you don't learn to "tune out" the reminder. You can set it to go off at random times (like anywhere between 6 to 9 p.m.), and the alert will act as a legitimate reminder because you haven't trained your brain to ignore the message.

The key to this step is to **create an alert for the replacement habit**, not for the one you're giving up. That way, you don't get yet another reminder of what you're trying to give up.

CASE STUDY

My habit reminder was very straightforward. Between 7 and 9 p.m., Mind Jogger would send this alert: *"Put your cellphone on its charger in your office."*

In many cases, I had already completed the habit, so I wouldn't see this message until the morning. If I forgot to do it for some reason, then the message would act as a reminder to walk into my office and put away the phone.

PART III:

BUILD A SUPPORT SYSTEM

Step #15: Keep an Accountability Journal

Making a commitment to yourself is just *half* the battle. In all likelihood, you can't make a lasting change on your own. That's why it's important to build a support system of people who will help you follow through with this goal.

People can either make or break your success. When you include them in a habit change, you'll get assistance whenever you feel temptation or amoment of weakness.

The simplest way to get started with a support system is to maintain an accountability journal.

With this tool, you track your day-to-day attempt to change a habit, including every trigger, impulse or metric. The more information you include, the easier it will be to understand what causes you to do the bad habit.

Depending on the nature of the routine, here are a few things to include in an accountability journal:

- Number of times you do the bad habit
- Amount of time you spend doing this activity
- Total calories, broken down by individual foods
- Current weight and/or body mass index
- Feelings, emotions and impulses
- Challenges you're currently experiencing

EXAMPLE:

Let's say you want to quit smoking. Every day, you would set a maximum number of cigarettes to smoke. Then you'd record the amount you *actually* smoked as well as the feelings and impulses that led you to light up.

The key with an accountability journal is to provide 100 percent disclosure. You need to write down everything—*even* if you fail with your goal.

CASE STUDY

My bad habit didn't require a lot of accountability. As I've mentioned a few times before, either I put away the cellphone or I failed to do it. What I *did do* to be accountable was use Lift.do (http://lift.do/) to track this replacement habit.

With Lift, you create a profile and add the habits you'd like to build. What makes this app different from others is it has a social component. Members can monitor the achievement of other members. They can cheer each other on, send messages and generally help one another out. In essence, Lift offers a built-in support system of people who hold you accountable for your habit change.

Unfortunately, only five people participate in the "no cell phone before sleep" (https://www.lift.do/plans/86971-no-cell-phone-before-sleep) habit, but even this small amount of tracking helped me stay consistent.

Step #16: Make a Public Declaration

Social networks have become a major part of our daily existence, so a great way to harness these friendships is to ask for support on your habit change goal.

Nobody wants to look bad. Post updates of your habit change on social media account to get encouragement from your friends. Create a simple tweet or Facebook post, or use a mobile phone app like Lift.do. Lift automatically updates your account with progress reports.

Never underestimate the power of social approval. Simply *knowing* you have to be accountable for your actions keeps you focused on a habit change.

Part of the reason this works can be explained by a concept called the **Hawthorne Effect**.

The term *Hawthorne Effect* was coined in the 1950s based on a series of experiments originally conducted in the 1920s.

During an industrial experiment to see whether factory workers were more productive with a greater or lesser amount of ambient lighting, researchers found that the productivity of *both groups* increased from the control amounts. After further experiments, it became clear that this happened *because* the test subjects knew they were being studied.

The lesson here?

When people are being observed, they want to look good and perform well.

It is human nature. If we know we're being watched, it's natural to increase our performance and give that little bit of extra effort.

The Hawthorne Effect shows that we do better when we know we're being watched and reviewed by others. So to improve your chances of success, simply put yourself out there to *be observed* by others.

You can do this by making public declarations in five ways:

1. Tell your family and friends about your goals.
2. Post updates on social media sites like Facebook, Twitter and Google+.
3. Join habit-related online groups and find accountability partners.
4. Use habit-building apps (like Lift.do).
5. Start a blog or podcast that chronicles your habit change journey.

You'd be surprised at how well public declarations work. When you know you're being observed, you're more likely to follow through with a promise. Otherwise, you risk looking like a failure.

CASE STUDY

My "public declaration" for the cellphone sabbatical was this book. Last May, I set a goal to write a step-by-step process for breaking bad habits, and within this book, I wanted to provide a real-world example.

By committing to this goal, I knew I had to follow through with breaking a specific bad habit that I had at the time. Otherwise, I wouldn't have enough material to provide to you—the reader. Whenever I felt like slacking off, I reminded myself that one failure could become a slippery slope that prevented me from achieving my goal. This alone kept me focused on building the replacement habit.

Step #17: Find an Accountability Partner

A way to supercharge your replacement habit efforts is to meet with someone who shares a similar desire to change that behavior.

You can talk with this person a few times each week and share your experiences. If they live locally, you can meet in person to build the new routine together. This is a great strategy if you'd like to replace a poor health habit with regular exercise.

Another idea is to find a "sponsor" who can talk you through those moments of weakness. Simply call this person when you feel tempted and they'll help you overcome the challenge.

An accountability partner doesn't have to live nearby. It's not too hard to meet people on forums and Facebook groups who share a common interest. All you have to do is install a tool like Skype (http://www.skype.com/), and you can talk for five minutes a few times each week.

Finally, the Stickk tool (http://www.stickk.com/) provides a unique way to stick with a habit change. Here, you'll make a "Commitment Contract" to achieve a goal within a specific timeframe. The hitch is you have to invest money in this habit change. If you don't follow through, then your cash will go to the charity (or anti-charity) of your choice.

CASE STUDY

My accountability partner was my fiancée. Whenever she caught me using my phone, she'd simply remind me of what I wanted to achieve.

Often, all I needed was a simple "I thought you didn't want to look at your phone in the evening?" to make sure I followed through with the replacement habit.

Step #18: Ignore the Naysayers

Sadly, there *will* be people who will subconsciously (or consciously) try to sabotage your efforts at self-improvement. They could be random strangers, close friends or even family members. Their words can be poison because they'll flood your mind with self-doubt and limiting beliefs. Listen to their "advice" at your own peril. The moment you start believing them is the moment you'll take that first step towards failure.

Having a plan for handling naysayers is as important as knowing what to do when you're tempted by an impulse. You need to know *what to say* and *what to do* whenever a person says something that causes you to second-guess a habit change. My suggestion is to find a way to ignore their comments or <u>immediately</u> rebuff these statements.

This goes back to step #13, where we talked about if-then planning. If you feel like certain individuals are a source of negativity, then you'll need to create a plan for how you'll handle their feedback.

As an example, you could do any (or all) of the following:

"If my parents remind me of past failures, then I will politely change the subject."

"If I post a status on social media and get a negative response from someone, then I will either remove that person as a friend or "mute" their updates."

"If I don't get a positive experience from a habit-building tool, then I will download another app that reinforces my new behavior."

"If the people around me dwell in negativity, then I will start surrounding myself with more positive people."

Be very careful with the people around you. Forming a new habit is often a fragile experience. One negative comment can completely derail your efforts. If someone is a constant source of negativity, then it's time to rethink your relationship—perhaps even find a way to remove them from your life.

CASE STUDY

For the "no cellphone habit," the naysayers were the imaginary conversations I had in my head. No, I don't hear voices. Instead, since I get a lot of emails and social media messages, I had to remind myself that it was "okay" not to be available 24 hours per day, 7 days per week. I had to tell myself that most messages could wait a day or so for a response.

What I ultimately had to do was rethink my "daily inbox zero habit." Instead of forcing myself to respond to every single message, every single day, I focused on processing each message. Now, time-critical stuff (usually) gets a response within 24 hours. Everything else gets a response within 48 to 72 hours. With this shift in attitude, I no longer felt obligated to sort through messages late at night and worry about responding to each person.

Interestingly enough, I haven't had one person who complained that it took a day or so to receive a reply, so the naysayers in my head were nothing more than figments of my imagination.

Step #19: Avoid Trigger Locations

People aren't the only triggers for a bad habit. Sometimes a location can cause an impulse to follow a specific routine.

During the weeks while you're testing a replacement habit, try to avoid the places that might cause you to revert back to your old behavior.

For instance, many people smoke while they're drinking. So if you're looking to eliminate the cigarette habit, the best thing you can do is avoid the bar scene. Yes, this might mean ditching your friends for a brief period, but this strategy can help you minimize the impulses you'll feel to light up.

CASE STUDY

The trigger location for me is my home office. During the daytime, it's a relaxing place where I'm productive and able to get things done. At night, it creates the same sense of purpose. If I'm in the office, then I feel the urge to think about business and *do stuff.*

As a result, I had to learn early on in the replacement habit to avoid my office. Otherwise, I would either check my cellphone or hop on the computer to do "just one more task."

PART IV:
OVERCOME CHALLENGES

Step #20: Maintain a Healthy Lifestyle and Attitude

As I mentioned before, *ego depletion* can leave your willpower in a weakened state. If you're always tired, hungry, stressed or depressed, you're more likely to succumb to temptation.

A simple way to fight ego depletion is to live a healthy lifestyle. Since this problem is largely caused by a low level of glucose (or "low blood sugar"), you can fight temptation by:

- Getting a full night's sleep to feel energized in the morning.
- Staying hydrated by drinking at least eight, 8-ounce cups of water every day.
- Eating a balanced meal every day—including fruits, vegetables, (good) carbohydrates and lean protein.
- Carrying healthy snacks with you to eat when you feel hungry.
- Exercising to reduce stress and maintain an optimal weight.

Don't underestimate the power of the mind-body connection. When you live a balanced, healthy life, breaking a bad habit becomes that much easier.

(To learn more about this strategy, check out my Kindle book *70 Healthy Habits: How to Eat Better, Feel Great, Get More Energy and Have a Healthy Lifestyle* [http://www.developgoodhabits.com/70-healthy].)

Also, it's important to maintain a positive attitude about this behavior change. The trick is to know what to do whenever you have an impulse. When temptation strikes, reaffirm your commitment to stick to the new plan.

You can even recite a simple mantra whenever you experience a moment of weakness. This could be a silly phrase like "Smoke-free in three months," repeated on a regular basis. Say this over and over whenever you feel the urge to light up.

CASE STUDY

I feel fortunate that I enjoy getting regular exercise. When I felt like checking my cellphone, I'd do a few things:

First, in the morning, I reminded myself that any time spent on the phone would take away time from exercise and other aspects of my habit-stacking routine. Next, while working, I'd often take quick walking breaks instead of checking different webpages. In the evening, I'd remind myself that any time spent on the cellphone was time not spent exercising with my fiancée, reading or simply doing an enjoyable activity.

All of these actions helped me realize that being on the cellphone was literally robbing me of the one thing you never get back—time.

Step #21: Beware the "What-the-Hell Effect"

I know we've already talked about what-the-hell effect, but it deserves its own section because this attitude can often make or break your chances of breaking a bad habit.

On a long enough timeline, expect to make mistakes. In fact, you <u>will</u> slip up eventually. What you can't afford to do is have the attitude where a single mistake causes you to binge on the bad habit simply because you've already "failed" for the day.

Yes, tomorrow is another day, but it shouldn't be used as an excuse to go overboard on a bad habit.

For instance, let's say your goal is to smoke fewer than 10 cigarettes per day. Unfortunately, one day you slip up and smoke 12 instead. What you *shouldn't* do is have this attitude: *"What the hell, since I've already smoked 12 cigarettes, I might as well enjoy the day and smoke the whole pack!"*

The what-the-hell effect is a dangerous threat to your habit change. Whenever you slip up, simply accept the failure and focus on <u>minimizing</u> the damage. More importantly, never use it as an excuse to do more of the bad habit.

CASE STUDY

It sounds silly, but I had a simple mantra on those rare occasions when I slipped up and found myself wasting time on my cellphone. During these times, I would recite this phrase to myself:

"I will <u>only</u> check this page and nothing else."

This was a useful exercise because in the past, a single message or piece of information would snowball into 30 minutes of wasting time flipping through the interwebs.

By reciting the above mantra, I'd stay on course and only go to the one page that I absolutely had to check.

Step #22: Practice Streaking

One way to stay consistent with your replacement habit is to *practice streaking*, where you do it on a daily basis.

For instance, James Clear talked about how the "Seinfeld Strategy" (http://jamesclear.com/stop-procrastinating-seinfeld-strategy) can help you beat procrastination. The example he gave was how an aspiring comedian asked Jerry Seinfeld about his secret to success. The comedian told the following story:

"He said the way to be a better comic was to create better jokes and the way to create better jokes was to write every day.

He told me to get a big wall calendar that has a whole year on one page and hang it on a prominent wall. The next step was to get a big red magic marker. He said for each day that I do my writing, I get to put a big red X over that day.

'After a few days you'll have a chain. Just keep at it and the chain will grow longer every day. You'll like seeing that chain, especially when you get a few weeks under your belt. Your only job is to not break the chain.'"

The point of this Seinfeld example is simple—you don't worry about good or bad days. You don't wait until you're motivated. What's important is you show up every day and do the work. In other words, the best habits are formed by not breaking the chain.

The "streak habit" works because you create permanent routines. You don't worry about individual successes or failures. Instead, you focus on repeating the process day in and day out.

If you're an aspiring writer, you write every day. If you want to eat better, you stick to a sensible food plan every day. And if you want to be more productive, you complete a small list of your most important daily tasks.

It's not hard to form a habit when you have the "no-excuse" mindset. Simply focus on doing it—without fail—every single day and it'll turn into a permanent routine.

Now, one of the challenges with "streaking" is *what to do* when you experience days when you feel a lack of motivation.

Fortunately, Stephen Guise provides a simple solution in his book, *Mini Habits* (http://www.developgoodhabits.com/mini-habits).

One point he makes is it's hard to build new routines when you focus on massive outcomes (like starting with a goal to write for one hour instead of five minutes). He feels (and I agree) that it's better to make "micro commitments" and simply focus on doing a mini habit on a consistent basis. In other words, you focus on the streak, not the result.

As an example, let's say you'd like to reduce alcohol consumption by replacing your drinking habit with a walking habit. Rather than committing to a 30-minute walking routine, you'd set a small goal, such as a five-minute stroll around the block. That way, when it's cold, dark or rainy, it'll be easier to get out the door because your obligation is only for a few minutes.

Of course, your goal is to ultimately do more of the replacement habit. The hard part is building a consistent routine, so it's more important to stay consistent and complete the habit on a daily basis.

To get started with streaking, I recommend two apps. The first is Lift.do (http://www.lift.do/), which we've already discussed. The second is Chains.cc (https://chains.cc/), which is based on the "don't break the chain" principle. Try both and see which one works for you.

CASE STUDY

Consistency was an important part of the cellphone sabbatical habit. I used Lift.do for monitoring the action every day in June, only missing one of the thirty days.

At the same time, I also tracked a new habit: "read 15 minutes of nonfiction" every day. The idea here was to not only remove a negative routine, but to replace it with something positive.

Step #23: Forgive Yourself

A major reason people fail with a habit change is they don't know how to handle "falling off the wagon." Sure, they'll strictly follow a new routine for a few weeks, but they don't know what to do when they slip up. Many people use this mistake as an excuse to give up on the new habit.

At the risk of sounding like a touchy-feely new-ager, you need to *forgive yourself* when you miss a day or succumb to temptation. We all make mistakes. Beating yourself up over a slip-up is counterproductive to your long-term goals.

Again, let's go back to our discussion of the what-the-hell effect. If you make a mistake, the worst thing you could do is give up on your goal. Often, this will cause you to binge on the bad habit—which often leaves you worse off than before you started.

While it's important to be strict about a habit change, you want to avoid filling your head with negative thoughts. A mistake is a mistake. It doesn't mean you're weak-willed or lazy. It means you're human like the rest of us.

CASE STUDY

Fortunately, I only missed one of the 30 days in June. My excuse? I was working late into the evening and had to use my cellphone to manage a few things. And honestly? I wish I didn't cave in because I would have had a perfect streak for the month.

The important lesson is I didn't beat myself up for this slipup. Instead, I realized that I had to be better at managing my time at the end of the day. If it was close to quitting time, I had to learn to shut down and save work for the morning. After all, tomorrow *is* another day.

Step #24: Celebrate "Small Wins"

Breaking a habit can be a grueling experience. You can make it fun by rewarding yourself for achieving specific milestones. It's these "small wins" that will keep you motivated enough to stay the course and ignore temptations.

Small wins act as a progress point on your way to achieving a major goal. **For example, say that your main goal is to get out of debt.** This can be a daunting and discouraging task because it involves a lot of *moving parts*. So you decide the first step is to break the bad habit of excessive spending.

You could create a series of small wins like this:

1. Signing up for Mint.com (https://www.mint.com/) and creating a monthly budget.
2. Completing a 30-day "wait list" for a purchase you'd normally buy on impulse.
3. Building the daily habit of checking Mint to monitor your spending.
4. Paying off the balance of your highest-interest credit card.
5. Paying off the balance of your *second*-highest-interest credit card.

Each of these milestones is part of the larger goal of minimizing your spending, but they're broken down into manageable steps. Each also represents an achievement you can (and should) celebrate.

Now, the most important aspect of small wins is to avoid any incentive that's directly related to the activity you're trying to eliminate.

For instance, let's say you are trying to lose weight. Every time you meet a weekly weight-loss goal, you can treat yourself to a movie or a small shopping spree, but you'll want to avoid the all-you-can-eat buffet at Golden Corral.

Small wins make you feel like you're accomplishing something. If you focus too much on the habit you're trying to break, you'll never feel like you're making progress. By focusing on small wins, you'll have the motivation to keep going when you experience those moments of temptation.

CASE STUDY

Building the cellphone sabbatical habit was in itself part of a larger goal to improve my work-life balance. While I love being self-employed, it's often hard to turn off my entrepreneurial thoughts when I'm supposed to be relaxing.

So when I successfully built this one habit, I celebrated it with a nice dinner with my fiancée. I'll also admit that I took some guilty pleasure in watching a couple nearby who paid more attention to their phones than to each other.

Step #25: Focus on the Journey, Not the Destination

Don't worry about tomorrow or next year. Instead, focus on that next impulse, trigger or cue. Have a plan for what you'll do today and leave tomorrow for tomorrow.

With this mindset, you'll slowly make incremental changes. At first, you might not notice a shift in your habits. However, on a long enough timeline, you'll start to develop a permanent change to your routine. If you used to cave into a bad habit impulse, you now can resist this urge.

Habit development is like running a marathon. You can't start training today and expect to run 26.2 miles next week. But if you keep at it for a year, it's not hard to complete one of these events. The key to building any habit is consistency and daily action. Stay focused on what you need to do right now, ignoring what might happen in the future.

Finally, I urge you to consider breaking a bad habit the first step in a lifelong journey of self-improvement. Once you achieve your goal, think about other areas of your life to improve. It's likely you will never achieve true life mastery—after all, no one is perfect—but the process of replacing bad habits with positive routines will help you move one step closer to the things you truly desire.

CASE STUDY

Once I mastered the cellphone sabbatical habit, I looked for other "small wins" to improve my life. They included spending my days working on my top priorities, taking more time off and knowing when to let go of project ideas that really don't matter.

I'd estimate that I save about 30 minutes per day with this new habit. That doesn't seem like a lot, but over the course of my lifetime, this means I will have 7,300 hours—or 304 days—worth of extra time. That's an extra year I can spend pursuing new habits that further enrich my life.

As we close things out, let me ask a simple question:

Would you rather spend time on an activity that improves your life or on something that could lead to poor health, bad finances or reduced quality of life?

Hopefully you already know the answer to that question.

Final Thoughts...

Breaking a bad habit is an ongoing process that doesn't happen overnight. This book gave you 25 strategies to make a lasting change in your life. However, at the end of the day, they're nothing more than tips. In no way do they replace taking action and implementing this information.

Real results come from real effort.

Right now, you have a choice.

You could either close out this book, thinking all this stuff sounds good in theory, OR you could take immediate action.

My suggestion?

Read over this book one more time (remember it'll only take an hour to do it), take a lot of notes and then select that one habit you'd *really* like to eliminate. Finally, start tomorrow by taking aggressive action. Do this now and you'll be surprised at how quickly you see positive results.

Finally, remember that *any* type of habit change requires a daily commitment. Work hard, stay focused, track your results and learn how to overcome those moments of temptation. Like Henry Ford once said, "whether you believe you can do a thing or not, you are right."

Good luck on your journey of making lasting habit changes.

Steve "S.J." Scott

http://www.HabitBooks.com

Would You Like to Know More

You can learn a lot more about habit development in my other Kindle books. The best part? I frequently run special promotions where I offer free or discounted books (usually $0.99) on Amazon.

One way to get instant notifications for these deals is to subscribe to my email list. By joining not only will you receive updates on the latest offer, you'll also get a free copy of his book "77 Good Habits to Live a Better Life."

Check out the below link to learn more.

http://www.developgoodhabits.com/free-updates

Did You Like *Bad Habits No More*?

Before you go, we'd like to say "thank you" for purchasing our book.

You could have picked from dozens of books on habit development, but you took a chance to check out this one.

So a big thanks for downloading this book and reading all the way to the end.

Now we'd like ask for a *small* favor. **Could you please take a minute or two and leave a review for this book on Amazon.**

This feedback will help us continue to write the kind of books that help you get results. And if you loved it, then please let me know :-)

More Books by Steve

- *The Daily Entrepreneur: 33 Success Habits for Small Business Owners, Freelancers and Aspiring 9-to-5 Escape Artists*

- *Master Evernote: The Unofficial Guide to Organizing Your Life with Evernote (Plus 75 Ideas for Getting Started)*

- *Habit Stacking: 97 Small Life Changes That Take Five Minutes or Less*

- *To-Do List Makeover: A Simple Guide to Getting the Important Things Done*

- *23 Anti-Procrastination Habits: How to Stop Being Lazy and Get Results in Your Life*

- *S.M.A.R.T. Goals Made Simple: 10 Steps to Master Your Personal and Career Goals*

- *115 Productivity Apps to Maximize Your Time: Apps for iPhone, iPad, Android, Kindle Fire and PC/iOS Desktop Computers*

- *Writing Habit Mastery: How to Write 2,000 Words a Day and Forever Cure Writer's Block*

- *Declutter Your Inbox: 9 Proven Steps to Eliminate Email Overload*

- *Wake Up Successful: How to Increase Your Energy and Achieve Any Goal with a Morning Routine*

- *10,000 Steps Blueprint: The Daily Walking Habit for Healthy Weight Loss and Lifelong Fitness*
- *70 Healthy Habits: How to Eat Better, Feel Great, Get More Energy and Live a Healthy Lifestyle*
- *Resolutions That Stick! How 12 Habits Can Transform Your New Year*

All books can be found at
http://www.developgoodhabits.com

Made in the USA
Lexington, KY
11 February 2016